D1604717

Daily *warm-ups*

EVERYDAY SKILLS

Margaret Cleveland

WALCH PUBLISHING

The classroom teacher may reproduce materials in this book for classroom use only.

The reproduction of any part for an entire school or school system is strictly prohibited.

No part of this publication may be transmitted, stored, or recorded in any form

without written permission from the publisher.

1   2   3   4   5   6   7   8   9   10

ISBN 0-8251-5067-1

Copyright © 2005

J. Weston Walch, Publisher

P.O. Box 658 • Portland, Maine 04104-0658

www.walch.com

Printed in the United States of America

Table of Contents

Daily Warm-Ups: Everyday Skills

Math and Problem Solving

The *Daily Warm-Ups series* is a wonderful way to turn extra classroom minutes into valuable learning time. The 180 quick activities—one for each day of the school year—help students practice everyday skills in vocabulary, reading, and math and problem solving. They may be used at the beginning of class to get students into thinking mode, near the end of class to make good use of transitional time, in the middle of class to help students shift gears between lessons—or whenever you have minutes that now go unused. In addition to helping students warm up and focus, they are a natural lead-in to other classroom activities involving critical thinking.

Daily Warm-Ups are easy to use. Simply photocopy the day's activity and distribute it. Or make a transparency of the activity and project it on the board. You may want to use the activities for extra credit points or as a check on your students' skills as they are acquired and built over time.

However you choose to use them, *Daily Warm-Ups* are a convenient and useful supplement to your regular class lessons. Make every minute of your class time count!

Vocabulary

Health, Nutrition, and Medicine

Healthy Places

Where do you go for health care? Some people go to a doctor's office. Others may go to a clinic. A **clinic** is a place where you can get health care when you are sick. It is also a place where you can get advice on ways to stay healthy. What types of workers might you meet at a clinic? Can you think of three different types? List them on the lines below.

_____

_____

_____

_____

_____

_____

1

The Best Medicine

When you prevent something, you stop it. **Prevention** means stopping something bad, such as disease. In health care, prevention means that you practice healthy habits to prevent you from getting diseases. Can you think of five ways you might stop disease from happening? Eating well is one way. In the circles below, write other ways you can think of to prevent disease.

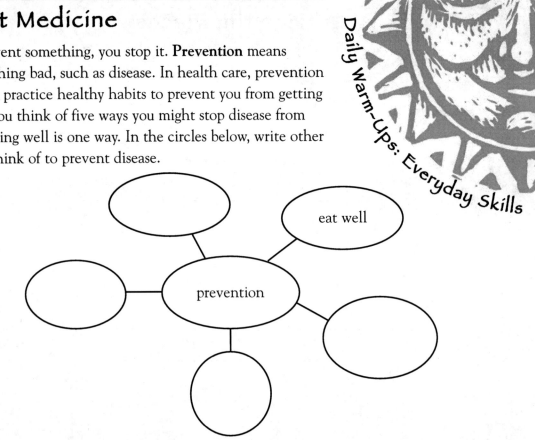

2

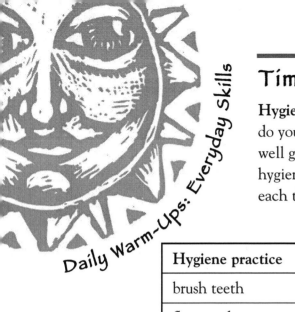

Time for Hygiene

Hygiene means practicing good habits to keep you healthy. How do you do that? One of the best ways is to keep yourself clean and well groomed. Below are several things to do to practice good hygiene. Next to each item, write how often you should do each thing.

Hygiene practice	How often
brush teeth	2–3 times per day
floss teeth	
wash hands	
shower	
comb or brush hair	
put on deodorant	
put on clean clothes	

3

Five Ways to Fitness

Fitness means having strong bones and muscles. When you are fit, it means that you feel healthy and strong. There are many ways to get fit. Ask five people you know to tell you how they practice fitness. Then write their answers on the lines below.

4

Five Ways to Fitness

How I practice fitness: _____

How others stay fit:

_____

_____

_____

_____

_____

Daily Warm-Ups: Everyday Skills

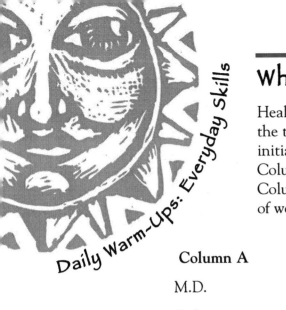

Who's Who at the Doctor's?

Health-care workers often have initials after their names that tell the type of work they do. In column A below, you'll see a list of initials that you might find after health care workers' names. Column B has the types of workers listed. Draw a line between Column A and Column B to match the initials with the type of worker.

Column A	Column B
M.D.	Licensed Social Worker
D.O.	Physician's Assistant
R.N.	Medical Doctor
C.N.A.	Nurse Practitioner
L.S.W.	Doctor of Osteopathy
P.A.	Registered Nurse
N.P.	Certified Nurse's Assistant

5

Special Doctors

A **specialist** is a doctor who specializes in one type of medicine. Read the list of specialists below and the areas they treat. Then answer the questions that follow.

dermatologist: skin

ophthalmologist: eyes

pediatrician: children

podiatrist: feet

ENT: ears, nose, and throat

orthopedist: bones and joints

gynecologist: women's reproductive system

6

1. You have a broken ankle. You see a(n) _____.

2. Your child has a cough that won't go away. You see a(n) _____.

3. You notice your eyesight is a little fuzzy. You see a(n) _____.

4. You are a woman and need a pelvic exam. You see a(n) _____.

5. You notice a rash on your arm that won't go away. You see a(n)

    _____.

Watch Out!

When a disease is **infectious,** it is spread by germs passing from one person to another. On the lines below, can you list at least five diseases that are infectious?

_____

_____

_____

_____

_____

7

Prevention List

If a disease is **contagious,** it means that it spreads quickly from one person to another. If you have a contagious disease, such as the flu or a bad cold, how might you prevent it from spreading quickly? On the lines below, list three things you can do.

Daily Warm-Ups: Everyday Skills

_____

_____

_____

8

Keep It to Yourself

People used to say that when you have a contagious disease, you should put your hand over your mouth when you cough or sneeze. Research has shown that diseases don't spread as quickly if you cough or sneeze into the crook of your arm. Why do you think it's better to cough into your arm rather than your hand? Write your answer on the lines below.

_____

_____

_____

_____

9

Where to Find Out More

Some diseases are very dangerous. AIDS, hepatitis, and STDs, also known as sexually transmitted diseases, are serious diseases. In some cases, they can even lead to death. It is important to find out more about these diseases and how they can spread. Where are four places you could go to find out more about these diseases? List them on the lines below.

_____

_____

_____

_____

10

Daily Warm-Ups: Everyday Skills

Food Diary

Good nutrition means eating foods that are good for you. One way to be sure that you are getting the right foods is to keep a diary of what you eat. Once you see what you are eating, you will be able to tell what you need to add or take away from your daily foods. Fill in the chart below by listing what you have eaten in the last 24 hours.

Breakfast	Snack	Lunch
Snack	Dinner	Snack

11

Good Nutrients

A **nutrient** is a food that helps your body grow and gives you energy. Put a check mark (✔) next to the foods below that you think are nutrients that are good for you.

carrot	_____	jelly beans	_____
roast beef	_____	orange juice	_____
hamburger	_____	broccoli	_____
butter	_____	egg	_____
cupcake	_____	ice cream	_____
milk	_____	popcorn	_____
cola	_____	fudge	_____

12

Daily Warm-Ups: Everyday Skills

The "N" Words

The following words deal with healthy eating:

nutrition   nutriment   nutritive

nutrient   nourishing

First find out the meaning of each of these words. Then use each word in a sentence. You may ask someone or look up the words in the dictionary to find their meanings. Write your sentences on the lines below.

13

ABCs of Vitamins

Vitamins are important to your health. There are several different types of vitamins that are found in foods. You can also take them every day in a pill form. The following is a list of vitamins normally found in your foods. See if you can find at least one food that has each of these vitamins. Write the foods on the lines below.

a. Vitamin A   _____

b. Vitamin B   _____

c. Vitamin C   _____

d. Vitamin D   _____

e. Vitamin E   _____

Ingredients

Ingredients are the items that make up the foods we eat. For example, ingredients that go into bread might include wheat flour, salt, oats, and soybean oil. Why do you think ingredients might be listed on packages of food? Write your answer on the lines below.

_____

_____

_____

_____

_____

15

Water, the Essential Nutrient

Did you know that much of your body is made up of water?

Fill in the following statement:

It is important to drink plenty of water because _____

_____.

Daily Warm-Ups: Everyday Skills

16

Health, Nutrition, and Medicine

Protein Power

Our food is divided into three groups—proteins, carbohydrates, and fats. Proteins are important for building strong bones and muscles. Below is a list of foods that contain protein. Check off the ones that you like to eat.

☐ beef   ☐ tofu

☐ fish   ☐ peanut butter

☐ chicken   ☐ nuts

☐ eggs   ☐ milk

☐ cheese   ☐ yogurt

Can you think of any other proteins that you like to eat? Write them below.

_____

_____

_____

17

© 2005 Walch Publishing

Carb Power

Carbohydrates are foods that give you energy. Healthy carbohydrates fill you up and have lots of vitamins and nutrients. But there are some carbohydrates that are not good for you. Put a check mark (✔) in the box next to the carbohydrates below that you think are the healthiest for you.

☐ rice   ☐ potatoes

☐ soda   ☐ bread

☐ squash   ☐ cookies

☐ pasta (noodles)   ☐ cereal

☐ brownies   ☐ peas

☐ marshmallows

18

Fats Are Great!

There are foods that contain good fats, and there are foods that contain bad fats. Good fats are found in olive oil, fish oils, soybeans, and canola oil. Find out at least three meals that could contain each of these types of healthy fats. List them below.

_____

_____

_____

_____

_____

Wellness Counts

It is important to keep yourself well by eating good foods and by getting exercise. But it is also important to be well in other ways. What other ways do you think are important? How do you keep well in these ways? Write your answers on the lines below.

Daily Warm-Ups: Everyday Skills

20

Tooth Doctor

A **dentist** is a doctor who takes care of your teeth. Imagine you are a dentist, and it is your job to tell your patients how to care for their teeth in between their visits to you. What will you tell them to do every day to care for their teeth? Write your answer on the lines below.

_____

_____

_____

_____

_____

21

© 2005 Walch Publishing

911

If there is an emergency at your house, you should dial 911. Think of an emergency that might happen at your house. After you dial 911, what will you say to the operator who answers the phone? Write your answer on the lines below.

Daily Warm-Ups: Everyday Skills

22

Emergency Vehicle

Complete the sentence below by circling the letter of the word that best fits in the sentence.

The name of the emergency vehicle that takes an injured or a sick person to the hospital is called a(n) _____.

a. fire truck   b. ambulance   c. bicycle   d. SUV

Now, use the word you chose in a sentence of your own. Write the sentence below.

_____

_____

23

© 2005 Walch Publishing

ER

The Emergency Room, or **ER**, of a hospital is where you go if you are very sick or if you are injured. What do you think happens in an emergency room? Share your answers with your classmates.

Daily Warm-Ups: Everyday Skills

24

Warning Words

Look at the words written inside the boxes below. What do they all have in common? Write what they have in common in the middle box.

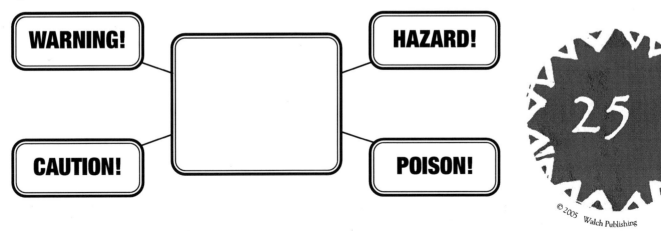

WARNING!

HAZARD!

CAUTION!

POISON!

25

First Aid

First aid is help that you give someone as soon as they have been hurt—before going to the doctor. A first-aid kit is a package of things that you might need to help someone who gets hurt. The list of items below might be found in a first-aid kit. On the lines below, tell what each item might be used for.

1. Band-Aids _____

2. first-aid cream _____

3. tweezers _____

4. scissors _____

5. tape _____

6. Ace bandage _____

26

Daily Warm-Ups: Everyday Skills

Hazards at Home

Dr. Milton works in the ER. She says that many people come to the ER because they have fallen at home and hurt themselves. Dr. Milton has some suggestions about how to avoid falling at home. What do you think are some of Dr. Milton's suggestions? Write them below.

_____

_____

_____

_____

27

Disaster

A **disaster** is a sudden, terrible event that usually causes great loss or damage to people and their belongings. A flood, a hurricane, and an airplane crash are all disasters. But today, communities have ways to try to prevent or help in disasters. On the lines below, name one or two ways in which your community is prepared for a disaster.

_____

_____

Daily Warm-Ups: Everyday Skills

28

The American Red Cross

The **American Red Cross** is an organization of people who help those who are touched by disaster. Imagine there was a flood in your town. How do you think the American Red Cross might be able to help? Write your answer below, or draw a picture that shows what the American Red Cross might do.

29

Learn the Meaning: Flammable

Read the following sentence and try to figure out what the word **flammable** means. Then check the correct meaning from the list below.

Don't light a match near gasoline—it is highly flammable!

___ smells very strong

___ is easily spilled

___ is easily set on fire

___ will make you sick if you drink it

Daily Warm-Ups: Everyday Skills

30

Daily Warm-Ups: Everyday Skills

Create an Emergency Health Information Card

In an accident or a disaster, an Emergency Health Information Card tells those helping you what you need. Below is a list of information that should go on your card. Fill in the card, and then copy it. Put it in places you use every day, such as your wallet, your backpack, your car, or your wheelchair pack.

Emergency Health Information Card

Name: _____

Personal support contact: _____

Medications: _____ Dosage: _____

Where located: _____

Allergies: _____

Adaptive equipment needed: _____

Special communication needs: _____

31

© 2005 Walch Publishing

Daily Warm-Ups: Everyday Skills

Practice Communicating

An emergency or a disaster can be upsetting because it is unexpected. You need to be prepared in case something ever happens. Be sure you know how to give directions quickly to someone who may be helping you. For example, if you use insulin, you might need to tell someone: "Get the insulin from the refrigerator door." Or if you use a wheelchair, you might need to say, "Get my wheelchair from the bedroom."

32

How could you direct someone to help you in an emergency? Write the words below, and practice saying them clearly so a helper can work fast to get what you need.

Command: _____.

Utility Checklist

A **utility** is a service that you use in your home to make your home run smoothly. Electricity, water, telephone, and gas are all utilities. In case of an emergency, you may need to be able to shut off your water, gas, or electricity. Do you know how to do that? With your class, go over what you need to do to shut off these utilities. Write the information on the lines below. Then locate these utility shutoffs at your home. Be sure you know how to turn them on and off.

Insurance

Medical bills and hospital visits can be expensive! That is why people buy **health insurance**. Insurance is money that you pay each month to a company who will then pay for your medical or emergency bills. Why do you think it is a good idea to buy insurance? Write your answer on the lines below.

Daily Warm-Ups: Everyday Skills

34

_____

_____

Making Choices

Every day you face important decisions about how to spend or save your money. These choices are called **alternatives.**

Imagine you have a choice between buying a new pair of shoes or going out for dinner. On the lines below, write which alternative you would choose and why.

_____

Why? _____

_____

© 2005 Walch Publishing

I'll Take It!

Choosing how to spend your money is hard. It's even harder if you find you can't resist spontaneous buys. **Spontaneous** means last-minute or spur-of-the-moment. But spontaneous buys can add up. If you spend too much money on them, soon you'll find that you don't have much money left. On the lines below, name some things that you have bought spontaneously.

_____

_____

_____

36

What happened as a result of buying these things?

_____

_____

Income

Income is another word for money that you earn. Answer these three questions about your income. You do not need to share your answers.

1. Where does your income come from now?_____

_____

2. Where will your income come from six months from now? _____

_____

3. Do you want to become financially independent?

_____

Why? _____

_____

37

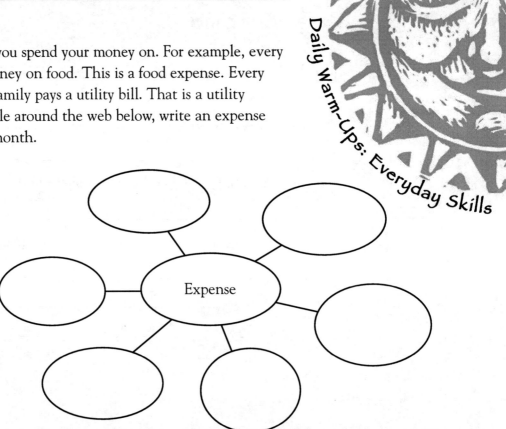

Expense

An **expense** is what you spend your money on. For example, every month you spend money on food. This is a food expense. Every month, you or your family pays a utility bill. That is a utility expense. In each circle around the web below, write an expense you may have each month.

Expense

Daily Warm-Ups: Everyday Skills

38

Daily Warm-Ups: Everyday Skills

Credit

A lot of people use **credit** to buy things they need or want. When you use credit, you are borrowing money from a credit card company such as VISA™ or MasterCard™. Then you can buy what you want when you want it and pay the credit card company back over a period of time. The company then charges you extra money to borrow from them. Credit cards have good things about them, and they have bad things about them. Make a list below of the good and bad things about credit cards.

Good things

_____

_____

_____

_____

_____

Bad things

_____

_____

_____

_____

_____

39

© 2005 Walch Publishing

Cash Flow

Cash flow is the amount of money you have to use each month. It is different from income. It describes the flow of money that comes in and goes out every month. When you get paid, you need to be sure that your money will last as long as you need it all month. For some people, getting paid only once a month makes for a difficult cash flow. Why do you think this is? Write your answers on the lines below.

40

_____

_____

_____

_____

_____

Bank Account

When you put your money in a bank, you set up an account. An **account** is like a folder that holds your money. It also keeps track of what you do with your account. Why do you think it might be better to put your money in an account at the bank rather than keep it at home? Write your answer on the lines below.

_____

_____

_____

41

Checking Account

There are two main types of accounts that people set up with a bank. One of them is called a **checking account.** When you use your checking account, you write an official note on paper, called a **check.** The check tells how much money you want to give a person, business, or store. It also has a place on it for you to sign your name. It is very important to keep track of the checks you write to people. Why do you think that is? Write your answer on the lines below.

42

Savings Account

Another type of account you might set up in a bank is called a **savings account.** This account is where you put money that you want to save. You won't use this account to write checks. The best thing about a savings account is that the bank pays you to keep your money with them. Can you name three reasons why you might want to set up a savings account?

1. _____

2. _____

3. _____

43

Bank Statement

Every month, the bank sends you a letter that tells you all the things that have happened to your checking and savings accounts during the month. This letter is called a **statement.** When the statement arrives, what do you think you should do with it? Discuss your answer with your class.

Daily Warm-Ups: Everyday Skills

44

Interest-ing

The money that the bank pays you to keep your money in your savings account is called **interest.** The more money you save, the more interest you get.

How is interest different from income? Write your answer on the lines below.

_____

_____

_____

_____

_____

Debt or Debit?

When you spend more money than you have, you are in **debt.** This means that you owe money back to your own account or to someone else. When you say *"debt,"* you don't pronounce the *"b."*

When you withdraw money from your account, the withdrawal is called a **debit.** Sometimes banks will give you a debit card to go with your checking account. This is a card that you can use to buy things instead of writing a check.

Daily Warm-Ups: Everyday Skills

Fill in the sentence below using the words *debit* and *debt.*

If you use your _____ card too much, you may go into _____.

Store Departments

Grocery stores have several different areas where food items are kept. These areas are called **departments.** In Column A below, you'll see a list of departments in a grocery store. In Column B, you'll see a list of foods you might find in these departments. Draw a line between the department in Column A and the food in Column B.

Column A

dairy

deli

produce

bakery

frozen

Column B

sliced turkey

ice cream

milk

bread

lettuce

47

Cashing Out

When you pay for your goods at a store, you check out with a **cashier.** What word is part of cashier that makes it easy to remember? Explain your answer on the lines below.

_____

_____

_____

_____

Daily Warm-Ups: Everyday Skills

48

Save Your Receipt

When you pay for something at a store, the clerk gives you a **receipt.** This is a piece of paper that shows what you bought, when you bought it, and how much you paid for it. Why do you think it is a good idea to keep your receipt? Write your answer on the lines below.

_____

_____

_____

_____

_____

49

© 2005 Walch Publishing

Returning an Item

Sometimes you need to bring back an item to the store at which you bought it. When you do this, you are making a **return.** In the circle below, write as many reasons as you can think of why you would return an item.

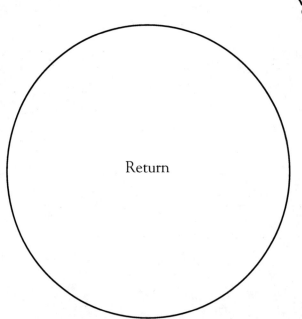

Return

Daily Warm-Ups: Everyday Skills

Clipping Coupons

A **coupon** is a piece of paper that offers you a company's product for less money than it would normally cost. Coupons are usually offered by the companies making the products. Why are coupons a good idea? See if you can come up with more than one answer.

1. _____

2. _____

3. _____

51

Sale!

Sometimes stores will put their items on **sale.** This means that the items cost less than they usually do. Why do you think companies put their items on sale? Write your answer on the lines below.

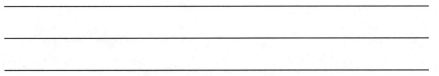

52

Daily Warm-Ups: Everyday Skills

It's a Bargain!

When an item goes on sale and you get it for a lower price than normal, you have received a **bargain.** Look at the prices of shoes below. Which pair is the better bargain? Explain your answer on the lines below.

_____

_____

_____

~~$35.00~~
$33.50

~~$45.00~~
$28.00

53

Rows of Aisles

Many stores are laid out so that you walk up and down rows, called
aisles. You don't pronouce the "*s*" in "*aisle.*" What types of stores
that you know of are laid out in aisles? Make a list on the lines
below.

_____

_____

_____

_____

_____

54

Daily Warm-Ups: Everyday Skills

Read the Ingredients

Ingredients are the items that go into the food you eat or cook. For example, when you make a peanut butter and jelly sandwich, the ingredients are the bread, the peanut butter, and the jelly. You buy the ingredients you need for cooking at a grocery store. What ingredients go into your favorite food? Make a list below.

_____   _____

_____   _____

_____   _____

_____   _____

Now write where you might find these ingredients in a grocery store.

_____   _____

_____   _____

_____   _____

_____   _____

55

Regional United States

The United States is divided into several **regions.** These are areas of the country. Find out the name of the regions of the United States, and write them below. Put a star next to the region in which you live.

Regions of the United States

_____   _____

_____   _____

_____   _____

_____   _____

56

How Far Away?

The distance between two places is measured in mileage. **Mileage** means the number of miles between one place and another. Speed limits are measured in **miles per hour,** which means how many miles one takes to travel in an hour. Miles per hour is often written as mph. Answer the following questions.

What is the mileage between where you live and where you go to school?_____

At about how many mph do you travel from home to school?

_____

Across the Country

Nationwide means "throughout the United States." Some types of transportation travel nationwide. You can drive nationwide or you can travel nationwide by other means of transportation. Can you name some of those other means? Write your answers below.

_____

_____

_____

58

Daily Warm-Ups: Everyday Skills

Travel and Transportation

All Around the State

Each state in the United States has a **border.** This is a line that separates one state from another. What states form a border with your state? Write the names of them below.

_____

_____

_____

_____

_____

59

© 2005 Walch Publishing

Legends and Symbols

Maps are often very small. So mapmakers use small drawings called **symbols** to represent areas. But how will you know what the symbols mean? Mapmakers create a **legend** that shows the symbol and then its meaning. What might happen if there were no legend on a map? Write your answer on the lines below.

_____

_____

_____

60

Roads and More Roads

Roads in the United States are connected nationwide. You can drive from the East Coast to the West Coast and go north and south by connecting roads. These roads are called **highways.** But there are many other names for roads. Write as many as you can think of on the lines below.

_____

_____

_____

_____

_____

61

Changing Planes, Trains, Buses

Read the following sentences. Choose the word from the list below that best completes the sentence, and write it on the line.

trip   send-off   tie

connection   shift   timetable

Not all planes, buses, or trains go directly from one place to another. Sometimes you have to change from one bus (or train or plane) to another. When you change, this is called making a

_____.

Daily Warm-Ups: Everyday Skills

62

Reading

Daily Warm-Ups: Everyday Skills

Finding Directions

Look at the direction in which the arrows are pointing below. Underneath or beside each, write the direction the arrow is pointing. Then, name one place that is in each of the following directions from where you are now.

North: _____

South: _____

East: _____

West: _____

63

© 2005 Walch Publishing

Map Symbols

Mapmakers often use symbols to show where things are. Imagine you are a mapmaker, and it is your job to create symbols showing where places are without using any words. In the space below, draw the symbols you might use for the following:

a picnic area

a hospital

a swimming pool

a road

a bridge

Daily Warm-Ups: Everyday Skills

What an Atlas Tells

Using an atlas of the world, see if you can find the types of maps listed below. Then tell what each map shows.

A **road map** shows _____.

A **vegetation map** shows _____.

A **population map** shows _____.

A **natural resources map** shows _____.

65

Where Are We?

Look at a map of the United States. List all the countries and
water masses that border the country.

_____   _____

_____   _____

_____

66

Daily Warm-Ups: Everyday Skills

Getting to Know the Neighborhood

Create a map of at least four streets in your neighborhood. Include any large buildings, parks, roads, or monuments. Be sure to include a legend to show what the symbols on your map represent. Then trade your map with a partner. Ask your partner to locate the various places you drew on your map. Draw your map in the space below.

67

© 2005 Walch Publishing

What's That State Like?

Look at a map of the United States, and choose a state that is far from where you live. Then look at the legend to find the symbols for the cities in that state. Now find the following things on the map:

1. The state capital (name) _____

2. The three largest cities (other than the capital)

    _____

    _____

    _____

68

Daily Warm-Ups: Everyday Skills

Daily Warm-Ups: Everyday Skills

Where's the Water?

Look at a map of your state. On the map, locate three rivers or
other bodies of water. Write their names below.

_____

_____

_____

The Biggest Cities

Looking at a map of your own state, locate the three biggest cities. Write their names below.

_____

_____

_____

70

Grand Routes

Looking at a map of your own state, locate three major highways.
Write their names or numbers below.

_____

_____

_____

Going HOMES

The Great Lakes are five very large lakes located in the northern part of the United States. Look at a map of the United States, and find these five lakes. You can remember their names this way: When put together, the first letter of each lake spells H-O-M-E-S. Fill in the rest of their names!

Lake **H**_____

Lake **O**_____

Lake **M**_____

Lake **E**_____

Lake **S** _____

Reading Recipes

Sections in a Cookbook

In each of the boxes below, you'll find the title of a section you might find in a cookbook. Below the boxes, you will find examples of recipes. Write the letter of each recipe in its correct section. You can check a cookbook if you need help.

Appetizers	Salads	Entrees	Desserts

a. chicken salad with almond

b. hot cheese wafers

c. old-fashioned apple pie

d. spinach pie

73

© 2005 Walch Publishing

Your Favorite Dish

What is your favorite dish? Find a partner or a group of people and discuss your favorite food. Then work with your partner or group to make a list of the ingredients you think go into your favorite dish. Then check a cookbook (or check with a chef) to find out what ingredients you might be missing.

Daily Warm-Ups: Everyday Skills

Favorite dish: _____

Ingredients: _____   _____

_____   _____

_____   _____

74

Making a Smoothie

Look at the following recipe, and answer the questions that follow.

Banana-Yogurt Smoothie
Serves 1; 13 g protein, 28 g carbohydrate

Ingredients:

1/2 c yogurt	1/2 c sliced strawberries
2 Tbl peanut butter	2 crushed ice cubes
1/2 banana	

Mix all ingredients in a blender. Blend until smooth and creamy.

---

1. How many people does this recipe serve? _____

2. What do you think "c" stands for? _____

3. What does "Tbl" stand for? _____

4. What cooking tool do you need to make this recipe? _____

75

What Should I Do?

Here are some directions you might find in a cookbook. Discuss with other classmates what each of these directions mean. Then write the meaning on the lines below.

76

a. Preheat oven to 350°: _____

b. Whisk together: _____

c. Toss onion with 1 tsp olive oil: _____

d. Fold chocolate chips into the batter: _____

e. Sauté vegetables until softened: _____

What Do I Need to Buy?

You are helping a friend make a dish for a party. Below is the recipe for the dish. From the recipe, write the ingredients you will have to buy at the store.

Tomato and Cheese Salad
4 firm tomatoes
1/2 pound mozzarella cheese
1/4 cup fresh basil
2 Tbl vinegar
3 Tbl oil
pepper to taste

Ingredients to buy:

_____

_____

77

Daily Warm-Ups: Everyday Skills

Using an Index

Cookbooks have an index at the back that lists all of the recipes in the book. The recipes are listed in alphabetical order. Look at the list of recipes below. Rewrite them in the order you would find them in the index.

meat loaf
zucchini-potato soup
scrambled eggs
chocolate cream pie
spinach salad
asparagus and almonds

Daily Warm-Ups: Everyday Skills

78

Low-Carb Eating

If you wanted to cut back on your carbohydrates, which of the recipes below would you choose? Explain your answer on the lines below.

Egg Salad
4 hard-boiled eggs
2 tsp mayonnaise
salt and pepper to taste
16 grams protein
1 gram carbohydrate

Beef Tacos
1 pound ground beef
6 taco shells
1 Tbl taco sauce
tomatoes, lettuce, and salsa
16 grams protein
12 grams carbohydrate

79

What Should I Do First, Next, and Last?

The order of directions in a recipe is very important. Otherwise, what you cook might not turn out well. Below is a recipe for brownies from a mix. The direction steps are out of order. Number the steps from 1 to 8 so that they are in the correct order.

_____ Bake at 350° for 25–30 minutes.

_____ Add two eggs.

_____ Add 1/4 cup vegetable oil.

_____ Preheat oven to 350°.

_____ Put mix in large bowl.

_____ Add 1/2 cup water.

_____ Pour ingredients into a greased baking pan.

_____ Mix together all the ingredients until creamy.

80

The Skinny on Soup 1

Look at the label on a can of black bean soup, and answer the
questions that follow.

Nutrition Facts

Serving Size 1 cup (242g)
Servings Per Container 2

Amount Per Serving

Calories 175   Calories from Fat 15

Total Fat 1.5g
Cholesterol less than 5mg
Sodium 730mg
Total Carbohydrate 30g
  Dietary Fiber 10g
  Sugars 2g
Protein 8g

1. What does the "g" stand for in the list of nutrition facts? _____

2. Which does the soup have more of: fat, carbohydrate, or protein? _____

3. How big is a serving size? _____

81

© 2005 Walch Publishing

The Skinny on Soup II

Look at the label on a can of black bean soup, and answer the
questions that follow:

Nutrition Facts

Serving Size 1 cup (242g)
Servings Per Container 2

Amount Per Serving

Calories 175   Calories from Fat 15

Total Fat 1.5g
Cholesterol less than 5mg
Sodium 730mg
Total Carbohydrate 30g
  Dietary Fiber 10g
  Sugars 2g
Protein 8g

82

1. How many calories are in one serving of soup? _____

2. If you ate the whole can of soup, how many calories would you eat?

    _____

3. What is sodium? _____

Daily Warm-Ups: Everyday Skills

Reading Labels

Prescription Medicine I

If you are sick, your doctor may order you some medicine from the drugstore. This order is called a **prescription.** The label on the bottle tells you key information about how to take the medicine. Look at the label below, and answer the questions that follow.

Rx# 76123   **Prescriber: Dr. Susan Blair**

TAKE ONE TABLET FOR PAIN EVERY
FOUR HOURS

> Take with food
>
> May cause drowsiness

TYLERTAB123 250MG TABLET

REFILLABLE 4 TIMES UNTIL 07/05/06
DISCARD AFTER 07/05/07

---

1. Who is the doctor ordering the medicine? _____

2. How often should the medicine be taken? _____

3. What can the patient do when the medicine runs out?

_____

83

Prescription Medicine II

Look at the medicine label, and answer the following questions.

Rx# 76123   **Prescriber: Dr. Susan Blair**

TAKE ONE TABLET FOR PAIN EVERY
FOUR HOURS

> Take with food
>
> May cause drowsiness

TYLERTAB123 250MG TABLET

REFILLABLE 4 TIMES UNTIL 07/05/06
DISCARD AFTER 07/05/07

---

1. What should the patient do if he or she hasn't eaten and needs to take the medicine? _____

2. What should the patient do if he or she has the medicine after 07/05/07?

   _____

3. Bonus question: What does Rx mean? _____

84

Daily Warm-Ups: Everyday Skills

Warning Label 1

You want to paint a chair that you found at a yard sale. You buy a can of spray paint. Look at the warning label from the can of paint. Then answer the questions below.

DANGER!

EXTREMELY FLAMMABLE.
CONTENTS UNDER PRESSURE.
VAPORS HARMFUL.
Use only with adequate ventilation.
Consult physician if reaction occurs.

---

1. What does "extremely flammable" mean? _____

   _____

2. What does "Use only with adequate ventilation" mean? _____

   _____

85

Reading Labels

Warning Label II

Look at the label from the can of spray paint. Then answer the
questions that follow.

DANGER!

EXTREMELY FLAMMABLE.
CONTENTS UNDER PRESSURE.
VAPORS HARMFUL.
Use only with adequate ventilation.
Consult physician if reaction occurs.

1. What should you do if you have a reaction to the paint?

   _____

2. Whom would you call if you had a reaction? (Give the person's name.)

   _____

3. What does "contents under pressure" mean? Talk with classmates to see if you
   can find out the meaning of that phrase. _____

Daily Warm-Ups: Everyday Skills

Daily Warm-Ups: Everyday skills

Ingredients

All foods that are packaged require a label that tells what ingredients go into the food. The ingredients are listed in order of how much is contained in the product. For example, if sugar is the first ingredient listed, then there is more sugar than anything else in the product. Look at the list of ingredients below, and then answer the questions about it.

Ingredients:
whole grain oats, sugar, oat bran, modified corn starch, honey, brown sugar syrup, salt, ground almonds, wheat flour, vitamin E

1. What do you think this product might be? _____

2. If you are allergic to chocolate, can you eat this product? _____

3. If you are allergic to almonds, can you eat this product? _____

4. Do you think this product has a lot of sugar in it? How can you tell?

   _____

5. Do you think this product is healthy? Why or why not? _____

   _____

87

OTC Medicines

OTC means "over the counter." These are medicines that you can buy without having a doctor order them. Read the label below for a child's medicine, and then answer the questions that follow.

Daily Warm-Ups: Everyday Skills

Child's Tummy Better	
Dosage:	
Children under 3	consult physician
Children 3–6	1/2 teaspoon
Children 6–12	1 tablespoon
Children 12 and over	2 tablespoons

Do not use for more than 2 days without consulting a doctor. In case of accidental ovedose, seek emergency help immediately. Shake well before using.

88

1. If you are caring for a child who is 2 1/2 and he or she feels sick, what should you do? _____

2. You give the 6-year-old you are caring for 2 tablespoons of medicine. Is this correct? If not, what should you do? _____

3. What should you do if the child you are caring for feels sick for more than 2 days? _____

Number Please

Most phone books are divided into three sections. Can you name these sections? You may need to look at a phone book to get your answer. (Some large cities may have a separate phone book for each of these sections.) Write your answers below.

1. _____

2. _____

3. _____

89

© 2005 Walch Publishing

Area Codes

The front pages of a phone book offer directions for communicating by phone all over the country. Among them are the area codes that you need to dial to get from one area to another for a long-distance call. Area codes cover a whole state or part of a state. However, a big city, such as New York City or Boston, may have more than one area code. Use the phone book to find out what area code numbers you would have to dial if you wanted to call a friend in these cities:

1. Annapolis, Maryland _____
2. Tampa, Florida _____
3. Washington, D.C. _____
4. San Diego, CA _____
5. Boise, Idaho _____
6. Flagstaff, AR _____

90

Community Services

In the front of your phone book, numbers are listed for Community Services. These numbers are listed alphabetically by service. Look at the list of services below. Then look in your phone book. Below, write one organization listed under each service.

Animal Welfare

_____

Children's Services

_____

Disabled

_____

Discrimination

_____

Education

_____

Family Services

_____

Health Department

_____

Housing

_____

Information and
Referral

_____

91

Daily Warm-Ups: Everyday Skills

Where Would I Find a . . .

The yellow pages list all of the businesses alphabetically by subject. This means that when you are looking for a dog groomer, you would look under "d" for dog. Then you would scan the pages to find the business you want. Below are three questions. You will need to use a phone book and/or the yellow pages to find the answers.

Daily Warm-Ups: Everyday Skills

1. Where would you go to find a new or used bicycle? Write the names and numbers of two places.

   _____

2. You want to arrange a nice dinner out with some friends. Find a restaurant, and write its name, location, and number.

   _____

3. You've decided you want to have a pizza delivered to your home. How will you decide which restaurant to call?

   _____

92

Daily Warm-Ups: Everyday Skills

Whoops!

You have gone with a friend to a movie. When you arrive in the parking lot, the two of you get out of the car, close the doors, and they lock. Whoops! You both realize the keys have been locked inside the car. Using the phone book, explain what you would do to get help. Write your answer on the lines below.

_____

_____

_____

_____

_____

93

© 2005 Walch Publishing

Information Please

You are working on a report for school, and you need to do research. Where in the phone book will you look for help with your paper? _____

_____

Write the number of the place in your area. _____

94

Daily Warm-Ups: Everyday Skills

Is it Long Distance?

Using your phone book, find out what towns around your city or town are considered long-distance calls. Write them below.

_____   _____

_____   _____

_____   _____

_____   _____

95

Not a Working Number

A thunderstorm knocks out your phone service. Using your cell phone and the phone book, who will you call to report it? Write your answer below, and include the phone number.

_____

Daily Warm-Ups: Everyday Skills

96

Late Night Call

You or a member of your household gets sick suddenly in the middle of the night. It is not serious enough to go to the hospital, but you need medicine right away. Using your phone book, how will you find out where to go to get medicine? Write your answer on the lines below.

_____

_____

_____

97

Where Do I Find My News?

The daily newspaper is divided into several sections. Usually the sections are separated by letters in alphabetical order. Read a newspaper from your area. Below, write the title of the sections you find.

Section A: _____

Section B: _____

Section C: _____

Section D: _____

Section E: _____

98

Extra! Extra!

Newspapers use short phrases set in large and bold type to attract readers to the articles. These article titles are called **headlines.** Look at your local newspaper. On the lines below, write at least seven headlines you see in Section A.

_____

_____

_____

_____

_____

_____

_____

99

Newspaper Index

In the bottom right or left corner of the front page of your newspaper, you will find the index of all the important information that is included in the paper. Using your local paper, find out on what page the following topics appear:

1. Weather, p. _____

2. Television, p. _____

3. Deaths, p. _____

4. Comics, p. _____

5. Editorials, p. _____

Daily Warm-Ups: Everyday Skills

100

Daily Warm-Ups: Everyday Skills

Top News

In most newspapers, the most important news of the day is located in the upper right corner of the front page. Look at a paper from today or sometime this week. What is the headline of the most important story?

Now read the article, and create another headline that could have been used for this story.

101

© 2005 Walch Publishing

Where Do I Find It?

Match the story headline in Column A with a newspaper section in Column B. Draw a line between the correct headline and section.

Column A

Local Boy Raises Funds to Help Homeless

Stock Market Looks Weak This Week

President Insists on Pay Raises for Teachers

New Cars Hit the Lots Tomorrow

Tennis Tourney Takes Toll on Thompson

Column B

Sports

Wheels

Local News

National News

Business

102

Daily Warm-Ups: Everyday Skills

103

Entertainment in the News

Using a recent newspaper, look up entertainment information and answer the questions below. Write the information you find.

1. What are three movies that are playing near you?

   _____

   _____

   _____

2. What musical group is playing somewhere in town during the next week?

   _____

3. What are four comic strips that appear in your paper?

   _____

   _____

   _____

   _____

4. What are three programs on television Wednesday nights?

   _____

   _____

   _____

Classifieds

The **classifieds** are pages of advertisements of things for sale by stores and by individuals. Sometimes classifieds are large ads. Sometimes they are many small ads that run for several pages in the paper. Locate the classified section of your paper, and find six different things for sale. Write them on the lines below.

1. _____

2. _____

3. _____

4. _____

5. _____

6. _____

104

Daily Warm-Ups: Everyday Skills

What's Going On?

Look at today's newspaper, and find the Local News section—usually Section B. Scan the headlines, and then report to your class five important events or stories that are going on in your community today. List them on the lines below.

1. _____

2. _____

3. _____

4. _____

5. _____

105

The Sunday Papers

On Sundays, newspapers print a much larger edition than they print the rest of the week. There are usually several extra sections. Look at a Sunday paper from your area. On the lines below, list four extra sections that don't normally appear during the week.

1. _____

2. _____

3. _____

4. _____

Daily Warm-Ups: Everyday Skills

106

Daily Warm-Ups: Everyday Skills

Letters to the Editor

Every day, newspapers print letters from their readers. These letters are from people who want their opinion shared with the community. Find the editorial page in a recent newspaper. What are two issues that readers wrote about?

1. _____

2. _____

If you were going to write a letter to the editor, what would you write about?

_____

107

What Time Does the Bus Leave?

Imagine you are traveling by bus from your hometown to visit a friend 20 miles away. How will you know what time the bus is leaving and returning? Check the answer below that best answers the question.

- ☐ You look at a **map.**
- ☐ You look at a **clock.**
- ☐ You look at a **timetable.**
- ☐ You call **city hall.**

108

What Time Does It Get In?

Look at the bus schedule below. Then answer the questions that follow.

	Read Down		Read Up	
Thorsenville	9:30 a	4:10 p	12:15 p	7:00 p
Varney	9:55 a	4:35 p	11:50 a	6:35 p
Blairstown	10:16 a	4:56 p	11:29 a	6:14 p
Russell's Landing	10:39 a	5:19 p	11:06 a	5:51 p
Kate's Crossing	1:05 p	8:55 p	7:30 a	2:15 p

1. What time does the bus leave Thorsenville and arrive in Kate's Crossing? Leaves _____ Arrives _____

2. You live in Varney and need to be in Russell's Landing for a noontime lunch. What time will you board the bus in Varney? _____

3. Friends tell you they'll meet you in Blairstown in time for a 5:00 movie. You live in Varney. What time will you get on the bus in Varney? _____

109

© 2005 Walch Publishing

Return Trip

Look at the bus schedule below. Then answer the questions that follow.

	Read Down		Read Up	
Thorsenville	9:30 a	4:10 p	12:15 p	7:00 p
Varney	9:55 a	4:35 p	11:50 a	6:35 p
Blairstown	10:16 a	4:56 p	11:29 a	6:14 p
Russell's Landing	10:39 a	5:19 p	11:06 a	5:51 p
Kate's Crossing	1:05 p	8:55 p	7:30 a	2:15 p

110

1. You've spent the night in Kate's Crossing but need to be home in Varney before noon today. What time will you board the bus in Kate's Crossing?

   _____

2. Which takes longer, going from Russell's Landing to Varney or from Varney to Thorsenville? _____

3. You live in Blairstown and have been visiting friends in Russell's Landing. How long will it take you to get home on the bus? _____

Don't Be Late for Class

Read the following school schedule. Then answer the questions that follow.

	Monday	Tuesday	Wednesday	Thursday	Friday
8:40–9:25	Reading	Math	Social Studies	Language	Reading
9:30–10:15	Math	Reading	Math	Reading	Math
10:20–11:05	Social Studies	Language	Reading	Math	Language
11:10–11:55	Lunch	Lunch	Lunch	Lunch	Lunch
12:00–12:45	Language	Social Studies	Language	Social Studies	Math II

1. On which days does Language class come just before lunch?

   _____ and _____

2. How much time do the classes take? _____

3. On what days does reading happen first thing in the morning?

   _____ and _____

111

Daytime Schedule

Look at the schedule, and answer the following questions.

Daily Warm-Ups: Everyday Skills

	Monday	Tuesday	Wednesday	Thursday	Friday
8:40–9:25	Reading	Math	Social Studies	Language	Reading
9:30–10:15	Math	Reading	Math	Reading	Math
10:20–11:05	Social Studies	Language	Reading	Math	Language
11:10–11:55	Lunch	Lunch	Lunch	Lunch	Lunch
12:00–12:45	Language	Social Studies	Language	Social Studies	Math II

112

1. On which day don't you have social studies? _____

2. On which day is there a special math class added? _____

3. How much time is there in between every class? _____

Daily Warm-Ups: Everyday Skills

Movie Going

Below is a schedule of times for all the latest movies. Look at the schedule, and then answer the questions that follow.

Rob's Revenge	(1030 130 430) 730 1030
O'Halloran's Gold	(100 400) 700 1000
Susan and the Susanettes	(1040 115 410) 725
Basic Powers	(1235 515)
Wishing for Summer	(1250 345) 645 935

1. What do you think the parentheses around some of the times might mean? _____

2. It's a rainy day, and you want to see a movie before lunch. What choices of movie do you have? _____

3. Which movie has no nighttime showings? _____

4. Which movie is probably the most popular? How can you tell?

_____

113

© 2005 Walch Publishing

Job Application

Look at the first page of a job application below. Then answer the questions that follow.

Maggie's Store
Application for Employment

Name _____ DOB _____

Address _____ State ___ Zip _____

Position Applied for: _____

SSN: _____

Year in School: Check one: Middle ___ High School ___ Adult Ed ___

If you expect to complete an educational program in the near future, please indicate what type: _____

114

1. What type of job do you think this application is for? _____

2. What does DOB mean? _____

3. What is SSN? _____

Perfect for the Job

Look at the second part of a job application. Then answer the questions that follow.

Experience: (most recent jobs first)

1. Title: _____ Duties: _____
   Length of time working: _____

2. Title: _____ Duties: _____
   Length of time working: _____

3. Title: _____ Duties: _____
   Length of time working: _____

References: Name: _____ Phone number: _____
If this is your first job, please explain experience you have had to apply for this position: _____
_____

---

1. Fill in the Experience part of the job application. Be sure to practice writing your job duties on a separate sheet of paper before committing your words to the application.

2. Why do you think employers want to see the most recent job first on an application?_____

3. What is a reference? _____

4. Whom would you write as a reference? _____

115

Check It Off

Look at the Reading Checklist form below. Then answer the questions that follow.

Reading Checklist

Name _____ Month _____

Books:
Title: _____ Author _____ Type: fiction nonfiction
Title: _____ Author _____ Type: fiction nonfiction
Title: _____ Author _____ Type: fiction nonfiction

Other reading (Check all that apply):
Magazines ___ Computer Screen ___ Road Signs ___ Encyclopedia ___
Poetry ___ Letters/e-mails ___ Dictionary ___ Maps/Atlas ___ Newspaper ___

116

1. For what kind of information does this form ask? _____

   _____

2. What types of books does it ask that you have read? _____

   _____

3. What do these different types of books mean? _____

   _____

4. What does the form ask you to do under "other reading"? _____

   _____

Daily Warm-Ups: Everyday Skills

How Am I Doing?

Below is a form to help you organize your assignments each week. Read the form, and then answer the questions that follow.

Assignment Sheet

Date	Assignment	Due Date	Completed	Late	Grade/Comment

1. In what way do you think this might be a useful form for a student?

   _____

2. In what way might this form be useful for a teacher? _____

   _____

3. Fill in the Assignment Sheet form above based on two or three assignments you have had in the past month.

117

© 2005 Walch Publishing

Renting a Bike

You would like to rent a bicycle for touring around a new town. You discover an online reservation form. Look at the form below, and answer the questions that follow.

BETTY JORDAN'S BIKE SHOP   RESERVATION FORM

If you want to rent a bike, please fill out this form, and we will get back to you within 24 hours. Or call 1-800-555-BIKE for reservation information.

NAME		ADDRESS	
PHONE		E-MAIL	

HOW MANY BIKES DO YOU WANT TO RENT? ☐

AGE AND APPROXIMATE WEIGHT OF RIDERS ☐ ☐ ☐

118

1. Why do you think the form asks for your e-mail? _____

    _____

2. What would you do if you realized you made a mistake on the form after you already sent it to Betty Jordan's Bike Shop? _____

    _____

3. Why do you think the form asks for the renters' weight? _____

    _____

Math and Problem Solving

Daily Warm-Ups: Everyday skills

Health, Nutrition, and Medicine

Cooking for a Gang of 12

You want to cook a dish that you can serve at a party for 12 people. You find a recipe that you like, but it says that it only serves 4 people. What will you have to do to make the recipe work for your party? Write your solution below.

_____

_____

_____

_____

119

Calorie Counting

You decide that you want to keep track of how many calories you should eat each day. You find a web site and learn that, for your current weight and activity level, you need 2,000 calories per day. You want to eat this amount over the course of the day, so you make up a chart. Finish the chart below. All meals should have the same number of calories, and all snacks should have the same number of calories.

Daily Warm-Ups: Everyday Skills

120

Breakfast	Snack	Lunch	Dinner	Snack
	250		500	

Getting the Right Dressing

You are making a special salad dressing that you want to serve now. You also want to keep some for later. You want to double the amounts called for in the recipe. Look at the amounts below, and figure out how much you will need to add to double the recipe.

1/2 cup mayonnaise   = _____

1/4 cup sour cream   = _____

3 tablespoons cream   = _____

3/4 cup fresh parsley   = _____

121

© 2005 Walch Publishing

Cooking for One

You are cooking just for yourself tonight. The recipe you want to make serves four. Below are the ingredients for your salad with cheesy salad dressing. Change the amounts so that the salad and dressing will serve just you.

122

Green and Red Salad

4 c mixed greens = _____

2 cucumbers, sliced and cut up = _____

2 tomatoes, diced = _____

1 red pepper, diced = _____

4 tsp scallions = _____

Cheesy Dressing

1 c fresh lemon juice = _____

3 c oil = _____

4 Tbl mustard = _____

1 c grated Parmesan cheese = _____

How Many for a Fill?

Your doctor has given you a new medicine. Read the instructions for taking the medicine below. Then figure out how many pills would be in your medicine bottle.

Take 1/2 pill two times a day for 3 days. Then take one pill twice a day for 27 days.

Number of pills in the bottle: _____

Packing Your Medicine

You are going on a trip and need to take your medicine with you. You decide that you don't want to pack the whole bottle. You are going away for a week. Below is the prescription information.

Take one tablet three times a day with meals.

How many pills will you need to take with you for a week? _____

124

Problem Solving Your Prescription

You are traveling to another city in a state far from yours. When you unpack, you realize that you have forgotten your medicine. You must have it. What will you do? Discuss it with your classmates, and write your answer on the lines below.

_____

_____

_____

_____

_____

125

© 2005 Walch Publishing

Minding Your Benefits

You have just taken a new job—congratulations! Your medical insurance will take effect exactly 90 days after your start date. You begin your job on March 10. On what date will your insurance take effect?

_____

126

Health, Nutrition, and Medicine

How Much More Will You Get?

You make $214 in your paycheck each week. Your company pays 90% of your insurance cost per week. You pay 10% of your weekly pay to cover insurance. How much comes out of your check each week to cover insurance?

_____

127

You're Perfect for the Job—Almost!

You are excited about a new job that you've been offered. Now you are meeting with the new boss to discuss your pay and benefits. She tells you that the job pays $9.15 an hour with no health insurance benefits. You really want the job, but you really want benefits. What are some ways you might solve this problem and still keep the job? On the lines below, write some ideas about how to discuss with your new boss about solving this problem.

_____

_____

_____

_____

128

Daily Warm-Ups: Everyday Skills

Health, Nutrition, and Medicine

Daily Value

Food labels not only contain the list of ingredients, fats, carbohydrates, and proteins, but also the vitamins and nutriments contained in the food. On the label is a list called **DV,** which means Daily Value. For example, a cereal may have 5% of your DV of vitamin A. This means that you have now met 5% of your need for that vitamin in a day. You still have 95% to go.

Look at the cereal information below, and answer the questions that follow.

Wheatolios

Vitamin A	15%
Vitamin C	10%
Vitamin D	25%
Calcium	25%
Folic Acid	50%

1. What percentage of vitamin A will you still need today? _____

2. What percentage of calcium will you still need today? _____

3. If you eat two servings of Wheatolios, will you have filled your needs for Folic Acid? _____

129

© 2005 Walch Publishing

Disaster Prep

Your area is threatened with a flood. The emergency radio station tells you to leave your home and to bring the following supplies. There are six people living in your house. How many total supplies will you bring?

Extra canned food for 4 days (1 can per person) = _____

1 blanket per person = _____

1 flashlight per person = _____

Extra batteries for flashlights = _____

3 water bottles per person = _____

2 changes of clothes per person = _____

130

Health, Nutrition, and Medicine

How Fast?

An ambulance is speeding to the hospital at 60 mph. The hospital is 6 miles away. How fast will the ambulance reach the hospital? Circle the correct answer.

    a. 10 minutes

    b. 6 minutes

    c. 3 minutes

    d. 20 minutes

131

What If the Bills Aren't Paid?

Name four things that could happen if you don't pay a bill on time.

1. _____

2. _____

3. _____

4. _____

Daily Warm-Ups: Everyday Skills

132

Is It Enough?

Your monthly income is $1,066. Your expenses are listed below. Answer the questions that follow.

Rent: $325
Food: $220
Phone: $32
Electricity: $23
Water/Sewer: $17
Car: Gas: $29
      Insurance: $87
Clothes/haircuts/misc: $60

1. Are you making enough money to cover your expenses? _____

2. Is there money left over each month? _____

3. What might be a good thing to do with the remaining money per month? _____

Interest Earnings

You have tucked away some money into a savings account. Right now, you have $550 in savings. The bank gives you 2.4% interest on your account. How much money will you have at the end of the month? Circle the letter of the correct answer.

    a. $570.40

    b. $550.00

    c. $552.40

    d. $563.20

134

Credit Charges

Every time you use your credit card, you are charged $2.23. If you use your credit card an average of 8 times per month, how much extra will you be charged? Write your answer below.

Per Month? _____

Per Year? _____

135

© 2005 Walch Publishing

Debit Charges

Your bank, which is across town, does not charge you anything if you use its ATM to withdraw cash. But the bank just down the street charges $1.50 each time you use its machine. If you use your ATM card 57 times a year, how much extra will it cost you per year to use the ATM closer to your home? Write your answer below.

_____

136

The Rent

Your rent should equal approximately one and a half week's worth of salary. If you are making $22,500 per year, how much rent should you be paying? Circle the correct answer.

    a. $349.04

    b. $449.04

    c. $549.04

    d. $649.04

137

© 2005 Walch Publishing

What If You Are Over Budget?

You have set aside $42.00 per month for your phone bill. This month you are surprised to see that the bill came in at $55.00. (It was your friend's birthday, and you called her long distance.) What can you do to balance your budget this month and still get the bill paid on time? Write your notes on the lines below.

_____

_____

_____

Daily Warm-Ups: Everyday Skills

138

Checking on Your Checking

Your bank charges you $.25 to process each check that you write. Over the course of the last six months, you have written the following numbers of checks:

November: 13
December: 22
January: 8
February: 10
March: 8
April: 9

What is the average amount you pay each month in check-writing fees? _____

Oops! You Bounced!

You made a mistake in your addition and thought you had more money in your checking account than you did. Then, you wrote a check to a store for more money than you had in the account. Your bank charges you $27.00 for the bounced check. The store charges you $25.00 for the returned check. You originally spent $14.50 at the store. How much will you end up paying all together?

Daily Warm-Ups: Everyday Skills

_____

What lesson have you learned?_____

Debit or Credit?

You go to the drugstore to buy some items you need. When you check out, the cashier asks you, "Debit, or credit?" What's the difference? Write your answer on the lines below.

_____

_____

_____

Taxes

In the last year, you have made $14,270. Taxes have been taken out of your pay at the rate of 8%. Circle the correct answer.

1. Assuming you've been paid every week, how much money in taxes has come out each week?

   a. $22.00

   b. $21.95

   c. $31.00

   d. $22.95

2. How much has your weekly paycheck been?

   a. $255.00

   b. $244.77

   c. $252.47

   d. $198.50

142

Handling Money

What If You Don't Have a Budget?

In the circle below, brainstorm at least five things that could happen if you don't keep a budget.

Uh-Oh! No Budget!

143

Price per Pound

When you buy quantities of items at the grocery store—meats, grains, nuts, fruits, or vegetables (all the good foods!)—the price is measured in price per pound. Imagine you want to buy 6 apples, and they cost $1.19 per pound. There are 4 apples in a pound. How much will you spend for the apples? Write your answer below.

_____

144

Shoes for Sale

Look at the ad below. Then answer the questions that follow.

Sheila Russell Shoe Outlet

**Buy one pair, get the second pair of similar
or lesser value 1/2 off!**

Handbags, socks, summer shoes, all 30% off!

Preview sale on all fall shoes, 10% off!

1. How much will you pay all together if the two pairs of shoes you choose are $19.99 and $17.99? _____

2. How much will you pay for a handbag that originally cost $14.95? _____

3. How much will you pay for socks that normally cost $4.99 for three pairs? _____

145

© 2005 Walch Publishing

Tax Time

You go shopping in a state that charges 7% sales tax. This is what your sales receipt looks like:

> 1 CD @ 15.99
> 3 prs. socks @ 1.99 ea
> 1 polo shirt @ 12.99
> 1 towel set @ 22.49
>
> Total due: $57.44
> Add 7% tax: $61.46

How much would you save if you went shopping in a state that had no sales tax?

_____

146

Daily Warm-Ups: Everyday Skills

How Much Is It?

You are shopping at a yard sale and see a lamp that you can't live without, priced at $8. Then you find 4 books that you want for $.50 each. And then you find some glasses that you could really use for $.30 each—you need six of them. What would be your total paid at the yard sale if you got everything for the asking price?

_____

If the yard salesperson told you she would give you 10% off, then how much would you pay?

_____

Where Do I Find My Food?

Look at the drawing of a supermarket below. Then write in one thing that you usually eat from each department. Circle the area where you usually find the best bargains.

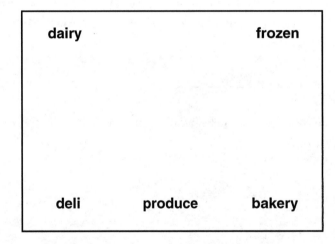

dairy	**frozen**
deli **produce**	**bakery**

Holiday Return

You receive some lovely presents for the holidays, but sadly, none of them fits you very well. You return the following items to the store:

1 blouse @ $8.99
1 sweater @ $15.00
1 flannel nightgown @ $12.99
1 skirt @ $9.99

1. How much money will you get back? _____

2. The store only gives you store credit, plus 15% for a post-holiday sale. How much store credit credit will you get?

   _____

149

© 2005 Walch Publishing

Coupon Clipping

On Sunday, the newspaper offers food coupons. Monday is your shopping day. Below is your grocery list with stars next to the foods for which you have coupons, plus the amount of the coupon. Read the list, and then answer the question that follows.

2 bunches of carrots @ $1.99/bunch
1 dozen apples @ $4.20/dozen * (10% off all apples)
1 head lettuce @ $.69
2 tomatoes @ $.59 each * (buy one get one free)
2 loaves of bread @ $1.29 each * (buy one get the second 1/2 off)
8 oz cream cheese @ $1.39
1/2 gallon of milk @ $2.40 per gallon

What is your total grocery bill? _____

Daily Warm-Ups: Everyday Skills

150

Lay-Away

You have finally saved enough money to put a down payment on a CD player you've always wanted. You will **lay-away** the remaining payments. This means that you will choose the CD player that you want—on sale—and then each month you will pay the store a little more money toward the player. When you have paid the full amount, you'll get your CD player! For lay-away customers, the store offers a 10% discount. The CD player you want is on sale at an 8% discount from its original $75.00. How much will you pay all together once you've paid off your lay-away CD player?

_____

151

© 2005 Walch Publishing

Chilly Winter

Your family has to buy oil during the winter months to stay warm. Each week the oil price changes. Some winters the oil prices go up very high. Look at the list of prices for Thomas' Oil Company from last winter. Then answer the questions that follow.

November: $.79/gallon
December: $.81/gallon
January: $1.01/gallon
February: $.98/gallon
March: $.87/gallon
April: $.84/gallon

152

1. How much did you pay if you bought 100 gallons each month? _____

2. Thomas' Oil Company offers you a seasonal rate of $.81 a gallon for all six months if you pay before winter. How much money will you save if you do this? _____

What If You Lose Your Receipt?

You need to return a can of soup to the grocery store because you notice that the can is bulging at the top. This could mean that there are bacteria in the can that could cause sickness. But you threw your receipt into the trash by mistake. What will you do? Write your answer on the lines below.

_____

_____

_____

153

What If Your Car Breaks Down?

You are riding on a highway with your friend and two small children. All of a sudden, you get a flat tire. You don't have a cell phone. What will you do? Write your answer on the lines below.

_____

_____

_____

_____

154

Making Connections

You are flying across the country! Your trip starts in New York City and ends in San Francisco, California. Look at the schedule below, and answer the questions that follow.

Lv. NYC	7:55 A.M.
Arr: CHI	9:59 A.M.
Lv. CHI	10:35 A.M.
Arr. SanFr	12:58 P.M.

Note: Don't forget there is three hours' difference between New York and San Francisco—one hour between New York and Chicago—and two hours between Chicago and San Francisco.

1. How long is the flight from New York to Chicago? _____

2. How long is the layover in Chicago? _____

3. How long is the flight from Chicago to San Francisco?

155

© 2005 Walch Publishing

Over the River and Through the Woods

You have been invited to your grandmother's house for Thanksgiving. Her house is just 2.5 miles away. You have decided that you will walk to her house. You can walk a mile in 20 minutes. How long will it take you to walk to your grandmother's house? Write your answer below.

_____

156

Itineraries

An **itinerary** is a plan of your trip. Imagine that you have been asked to travel from your town or city to Phoenix, Arizona. Create an itinerary of your trip on the lines below. You can travel by bus, plane, or train. Don't forget to account for time changes, if there are any between where you live and Phoenix. If you live in Phoenix, choose another place in the United States!

_____

_____

_____

_____

_____

157

© 2005 Walch Publishing

Budgeting Your Trip

A trip across country costs $625 round trip. You can save $25 per month toward your trip. How many months will it take you to save enough money for your trip? Write your answer below.

_____

Daily Warm-Ups: Everyday Skills

158

Budgeting Your Vacation Meals

The airfare for your trip costs $549 round trip. But you also have to plan for meals. Breakfasts will cost $4.00. Lunches will cost $4.50, and dinners will cost $6.00. You will be gone for a week. How much extra money will you need to take? Write your answer below.

_____

159

© 2005 Walch Publishing

Tipping Your Waitperson

When you go out for a meal, you need to tip the person who waits on you 15–20%. If your meal costs $12.49, and you want to leave a 17% tip, how much will your meal cost all together? Write your answer below.

_____

160

Travel and Transportation

How Far Will You Go?

You've decided to adopt a new pet from an animal shelter. First you drive to Animal-Luv shelter. It is 6.8 miles from home. Next you drive to Paws and Ponder, which is 7.4 miles away from home. Finally you come to Kitty Karma, which 10.6 miles from your house.

1. How far is Animal-Luv from Kitty Karma? _____

2. How far is Paws and Ponder from Kitty Karma? _____

(*Note*: Assume that you have traveled in a straight line from your home.)

161

© 2005 Walch Publishing

Off to Canada

You and your family are off to Canada. The Canadian dollar is worth $.78 in U.S. dollars. You buy a T-shirt that costs $15.00 in Canadian money. How much would this shirt cost you in U.S. dollars? Write your answer below.

_____

162

Tourist Treats

While you are away, you want to buy treats for your friends. You've brought $20.00 to buy treats for six friends. How much money will you be able to spend on each friend? Write your answer below.

_____

163

© 2005 Walch Publishing

What Do I Need to Know?

You are traveling to a foreign country. What types of information will you need to find out before you go? Write your ideas on the lines below.

164

Cabin in the Woods

You and your family have rented a cabin in the woods for two weeks. The landlord charges $450 per month for the cabin plus $6.00 per night per guest. You bring two friends for three days. How much will your family pay in rent all together? Write your answer below.

_____

Seeing the Relatives

You have relatives who live in Korea. You and your family have saved for a long time to visit them. What types of documents will you need to take with you to travel? Write your list on the lines below.

_____

_____

_____

_____

Daily Warm-Ups: Everyday Skills

166

The Price of Gas

You are traveling 120 miles from home. You buy gas that costs $2.04 per gallon. Your car gets 28 miles to the gallon. How much will you spend in gas to go 120 miles?

_____

167

© 2005 Walch Publishing

How Many Miles Is It?

You are having a busy day! You travel from home to school, but realize you forgot an important book, so you go back home again to get it. Then, you go back to school. After school you go home. Later, you go to the store to pick up some supplies you need for a project. On your way home, you stop at school for a meeting. Finally, you're home for good. Use the information below to find out how many miles you traveled today.

Home to School = 6.3 miles
School to Store = 2.2 miles
Store to Home = 4.1 miles

_____

168

Thank-You—Just for Fun!

How many ways can you say "thank-you"? What languages do you know? "Thank-you" is one of the most important phrases to learn. Here is "thank-you" in 11 different languages. Practice and try these new words out on your classmates.

Czech: Dekuji (Zhe-koo-yeh)

Greek: Euxaristo (Ev-kah-ree-stoh)

French: Merci (Mehr-see)

Hawaiian: Mahalo (Mah-hah-loh)

Italian: Grazie (Graht-see-yah)

Japanese: Arigato (Ah-ree-gah-too)

Korean: Kamsa hamnida (Kahm-sa hahm-nee-dah)

Russian: Spasibo (Spah-see-bah)

Spanish: Gracias (Grah-see-yas)

Swahili: Asante (Ah-sahn-tay)

Swedish: Tack (Dahk)

169

© 2005 Walch Publishing

What If You Are Lost?

What if you are traveling and you lose your documents, such as your passport, visa, and medical forms? Write your ideas on the lines below.

_____

_____

_____

_____

Daily Warm-Ups: Everyday Skills

170

Lost Suitcases

Say you are traveling by plane, and when you arrive at your destination, you find that your suitcases didn't make the flight. What will you do? Write your answer on the lines below.

_____

_____

_____

_____

Daily Warm-Ups: Everyday Skills

No Cash!

When you get to the checkout at the grocery store with your cart filled with food, you find that you don't have enough money to cover the expense. What will you do? Write your answer on the lines below.

_____

_____

_____

_____

Daily Warm-Ups: Everyday Skills

172

Daily Warm-Ups: Everyday Skills

No Cutting in Line!

Let's say you are standing in line and someone cuts into the line in front of you. You are in a hurry. What will you do? Would you say anything to the person, or not? Write your answer on the lines below.

_____

_____

_____

173

Bad Hair Day

What if you go to a new barber and he or she gives you a terrible haircut that you don't like at all. What will you say? Write your ideas on the lines below.

_____

_____

_____

_____

174

Overcharged?

What if you get home from a department store and discover that you have been overcharged by $18.00 for an item that was on sale. What will you do? Write your answer on the lines below.

_____

_____

_____

_____

175

© 2005 Walch Publishing

Doctor Talk

What if you go to the doctor, and she talks very seriously to you about a medical condition. The problem is that you don't understand all the words she uses. What will you do? Will you tell the doctor? Write your thoughts on the lines below.

_____

_____

_____

_____

Daily Warm-Ups: Everyday Skills

176

Turned Down for the Job

Let's say you applied for a job and, unfortunately, you did not get it. When the person who interviewed you calls to say you didn't get the job, what do you do? What can you say that may help you the next time you apply for a job? Write your answer on the lines below.

_____

_____

_____

_____

177

Just Say No

What if someone offers you a cigarette or an illegal substance?
What will you do? What will you say? What if the person is a
really good friend? Discuss your answer with your classmates.

Daily Warm-Ups: Everyday Skills

178

At a Friend's House

Let's say you go to a friend's house for a fancy dinner that she has spent a lot of time preparing for you. It turns out you really don't like the food. What will you do? What will you say? Explain your answer on the lines below.

_____

_____

_____

_____

179

A Big Windfall

What if you won the lottery? What would you do with the money?
Write your ideas on the lines below.

_____

_____

_____

_____

_____

Daily Warm-Ups: Everyday Skills

180

Vocabulary

1. doctors, nurses, front desk people, person to take blood, people who take X rays

2. Other prevention words include: exercise, get enough sleep, wash hands, get checkups, drink water, take vitamins.

3.

Hygiene practice	How often
brush teeth	2–3 times per day
floss teeth	1–2 times per day
wash hands	1–2 times per day
shower	1 time per day
comb or brush hair	1–2 times per day
put on deodorant	1 time per day
put on clean clothes	1 time per day

4. Answers will depend on learner interviews, but may include walking; running; lifting weights; swimming; playing any type of sports game, including tennis, basketball, wheelchair basketball, baseball, softball, kickball, and so forth.

5.

Column A	Column B
M.D.	Licensed Social Worker
D.O.	Physician's Assistant
R.N.	Medical Doctor
C.N.A.	Nurse Practitioner
L.S.W.	Doctor of Osteopathy
P.A.	Registered Nurse
N.P.	Certified Nurse's Assistant

M.D. → Medical Doctor
D.O. → Doctor of Osteopathy
R.N. → Registered Nurse
C.N.A. → Certified Nurse's Assistant
L.S.W. → Licensed Social Worker
P.A. → Physician's Assistant
N.P. → Nurse Practitioner

Daily Warm-Ups: Everyday Skills

6.
  1. orthopedist
  2. pediatrician
  3. opthalmologist
  4. gynecologist
  5. dermatologist
7. Infectious diseases include flu, cold, some types of pneumonia, measles, chicken pox, German measles, AIDS, hepatitis, sexually transmitted diseases, and stomach bacteria.
8. Answers include wash hands often, cover your mouth when you cough or sneeze, stay home when you are sick, try not to expose yourself to others.
9. Coughing or sneezing into your hand means the germs spread into your hand. Then you might touch another person or object that would easily spread the disease.

10. Answers include talk to a health-care worker, go the Internet and look up the diseases, look at a book from the library about health care, gather pamphlets from your doctor's office, take a class in health care and disease prevention.
11. Students should fill in the meals they have had in the last 24 hours. Help them discern between foods that are good for them and foods that may not offer good nutrition.
12. carrot, hamburger, orange juice, egg, roast beef, milk, broccoli
13. These words are fairly close in meaning. Be sure students can tell the difference between them, particularly their use as a part of speech. Nutrition, n: food and substances that fuel and provide energy; nutriment: n. any substance, which taken offers good nutrition;

nutrient, n: anything that nourishes; nourishing, adj: giving nourishment; nutritive, adj: describes a food that is healthy

14. a. carrots b. grains c. orange juice d. milk e. fish

15. Answers may include so that people know what nutrients they are getting; in case people are allergic to something in the ingredients.

16. Water moves nutrients around the body; water picks up waste from the blood and helps move it out of the body.

17. Students should check the foods they like best.

18. rice, squash, pasta, potatoes, bread, cereal, peas

19. breakfast: soy yogurt, cereal with soy, eggs sauteed in olive oil; lunch: large tossed salad with olive oil and lemon or vinegar dressing, tunafish salad; dinner: salmon, swordfish, bluefish, tuna fish; veggies sauteed in canola oil

20. Answers might include being well socially— by having friends and enjoying oneself; being well emotionally—having someone to talk to if one is upset; being financially healthy— having enough money; being healthy spiritually—having a place to go when a person needs support.

21. Brush at least twice every day; floss, and get regular checkups.

22. Tell the dispatcher your name, address, and telephone number. Also tell him or her exactly what the emergency is. Ask what you can do before emergency help arrives.

23. ambulance; sentences will vary.

24. Doctors work quickly to diagnose and help with sudden injury or sickness. Some typical

emergency room procedures include getting stitches for a bad cut, treating a broken or sprained arm or leg; treating people who have eaten bad food; treating people who have been in a car or bicycle accident.

25. They are all words to signal danger, be careful, watch out.

26. Band-Aids for cuts; first-aid cream for cuts and scrapes; tweezers to take out splinters or shards of glass; scissors to cut bandages or tape; tape to stick bandages onto skin; Ace bandage to bind a sprained arm, hand, leg, or ankle

27. Clean up any wet spots; use a sturdy stepladder if climbing or working up high; be sure all areas are clear of electric cords; shovel the sidewalk if there's snow; don't leave things on the staircase.

28. Some communities have sirens; others may have an emergency broadcast system to warn people of upcoming disasters; television stations broadcast storm warnings; some communities have the American Red Cross to provide shelters; if you live near a river or the seacoast, there are evacuation procedures in case of flooding.

29. The American Red Cross houses the blood supply; they provide shelter in emergencies if people have to be evacuated from their homes; American Red Cross volunteers help people who are wounded or injured in a large disaster; the American Red Cross can provide emergency medical care.

30. is easily set on fire

31. Students should fill out the emergency card. Discuss with them where they should keep their cards.

32. Even if there are no strong medical circumstances, students should know what they would say to an emergency worker to direct them to what they need in case of emergency.

33. Students should discuss their utilities and where they originate in their homes. Those who know about shutoffs should discuss their knowledge with those who do not.

34. In case of accident or injury that is very expensive, insurance may cover the costs.

35. Students might choose shoes because they are a longer lasting buy; they might choose dinner out if it is a special occasion. Be sure they have reasons to back up their choices.

36. Answers will vary; spontaneous buys can cause overspending.

37. If students are comfortable discussing their sources of income, encourage them to do so. Help them understand that the sources of income will change as they change work or make other choices.

38. expenses: rent, food, utilities (water, gas, electric), heat, clothing, transportation and travel, snacks, books, presents, entertainment (DVDs, music), medical expenses, school expenses, and so forth.

39. Good Things: You can get what you want or need right away and only pay a little over time; they are convenient if you don't have money with you; you can buy things over the phone or the Internet. Bad Things: It is easy to charge too much, then not be able to pay;

Daily Warm-Ups: Everyday Skills

you have to pay more money for every item you charge because of the extra money you pay the credit card company.

40. It is hard not to spend all of your paycheck at once; sometimes it is hard to hang onto your money for a whole month.

41. You could lose your money at home; someone could steal it; if something happened to your house—such as a hurricane or flood—your money would be lost.

42. You need to keep track of how much money you have in your account so that you are sure you can cover the checks you write.

43. Reasons might include: It pays interest; it allows you to save up money for emergency use; it allows you to save money for a large purchase.

44. Match what the bank says you have in your account to what you have accounted for that month. Be sure that the statement and your checkbook match.

45. Interest is a form of income; however, it is not earned by working, as income is.

46. If you use your debit card too much, you may go into debt.

47.

Column A	Column B
dairy	sliced turkey
deli	ice cream
produce	milk
bakery	bread
frozen	lettuce

48. Cashier contains the word "cash," which you can use to pay for something.

49. You keep your receipt in case you want to return an item to the store for some reason.

50. Reasons might include clothes didn't fit; don't like color; food package is open; discover that you don't need the item; item is a present you would like to trade in for another; you want cash for the item.

51. Accept any reasonable answers: You may be tempted to buy something you wouldn't have without the coupon; once you try the product, you may continue to use it.

52. Companies put their goods on sale to sell them quicker if they haven't sold; they may put them on sale because they are out of season; perhaps they need the space for new items.

53. The second pair of shoes (loafers) is the bargain. You save $17 by buying that pair.

54. grocery stores, some department stores, book stores, clothing stores

55. Students will tell about their favorite food. Encourage them to identify one or more main ingredients from their food. Then have them tell what part of the store they may get them from.

56. Students may choose some or all of the following regional delineations: New England, the Mid-Atlantic, the South, the Midwest, the Rockies, the Southwest, the Pacific Northwest, and the West.

57. Students may choose other places to measure mileage and mph. Help them approximate mileage between home and school.

58. trains, airplanes, and buses

59. Students should be able to identify the states that border their own state. They may need

Daily Warm-Ups: Everyday Skills

to look at an atlas or a map of the United States for clues.

60. Without a legend, you might not know what the symbols stand for.

61. freeway, parkway, beltway, street, lane, turnpike, route

62. connection

Reading

63. Encourage students to name one place that is each direction away from where they are now. Encourage discussion with others to figure this out.

64. Students may choose whatever they want to create for a symbol. They should be consistent about their symbols so that the map is not confusing.

65. A road map shows routes and roads; a vegetation map shows what types of plants grow there; a population map shows how many people live in a place; a natural resources map shows what types of products and energy are grown or found in a place.

66. Canada to the north; Mexico to the south; the Atlantic Ocean to the east; the Gulf of Mexico to the south; the Pacific Ocean to the west.

67. Students should be able to draw the major areas of their neighborhood. Instruct them to help one another read the created maps.

68. Students should find the largest cities of the state they choose; they should use the legends to locate the cities.

69. Students should discover bodies of water that include lakes, rivers, streams, ponds, or ocean.

70. First see if students already know their state's biggest cities; then they should look at the legend to determine which are the largest.

71. Students should look at highway numbers to determine the longest routes.

72. Huron, Ontario, Michigan, Erie, Superior

73. Appetizers: b. Salads: a. Entrees: d. Desserts: c.

74. Answers will vary.

75. 1. 1; 2. cup; 3. tablespoon; 4. blender

76. a. Put the oven on before you start cooking. b. Use a fork or whisk to stir in a quick circular motion. c. Pour 1 tsp olive oil onto a cut-up onion and stir until the olive oil has spread to all parts of the onion. d. Put the chocolate chips in and slowly stir them into the batter. e. Stir ingredient with oil or butter until it is lightly cooked—usually done in a small frying pan or sauté pan on the stove top.

77. 4 tomatoes, 1/2 pound mozzarella cheese, fresh basil; Point out that most households will have the oil, vinegar, and pepper already in stock.

78. asparagus and almonds, chocolate cream pie, meat loaf, scrambled eggs, spinach salad, zucchini-potato soup

79. egg salad because it has 1g carbohydrate

80. 1. Preheat oven to 350°. 2. Put mix in large bowl. 3. Add 1/4 cup vegetable oil. 4. Add 1/2 cup water. 5. Add two eggs. 6. Mix together all the ingredients until creamy. 7. Pour ingredients into a greased baking pan. 8. Bake at 350° for 25–30 minutes. Note: Steps 3, 4, and 5 can be arranged in any order.

Answer Key

81. 1. gram 2. more carbohydrate 3. 1 cup
82. 1. 170 2. 350 3. salt
83. 1. Dr. Susan Blair 2. one every four hours
    3. refill the prescription
84. 1. Eat before taking the medicine. 2. Throw
    out the medicine. 4. Rx means prescription—
    it literally comes from Latin and means
    "recipe."
85. 1. easily catches on fire 2. Use in a place
    where there is much fresh air
86. 1. Call your doctor. 2. Students should
    identify the doctor they would call. 3. The
    paint in the can comes out quickly.
87. 1. The product is cereal. 2. Yes, chocolate is
    not listed in the ingredients. 3. No, almonds
    are listed in the ingredients. 4. Yes, sugar is
    listed as the second ingredient. 5. It might be
    healthy because of the whole grains, but it has
    sugar, honey, and corn syrup in it, which is a
    lot of sweets.
88. 1. Call a doctor. 2. No, call 911. 3. Go call
    a doctor.
89. residential, business, and yellow pages
90.
1.	443	3.	202	5.	208
2.	813	4.	619	6.	928

91. Answers will vary depending on the
    community listings—these services should be
    found in most areas: Animal Welfare: Animal
    Refuge; Children's Services: Department of
    Human Services; Disabled: State Center on
    Deafness; Discrimination: Human Rights
    Commission; Education: Literacy Volunteers;
    Family Services: Community Counseling;
    Health Department: Disease Control;
    Housing: Homeless Crisis Hotline;

Information and Referral: Department of Corrections Legal Services.

92. 1. Students should look up "bicycle" in the yellow pages and discover two places that say that they sell bicycles. 2. Students can look up restaurants and peruse the listings. Encourage them to choose a restaurant that reflects their tastes. 3. Students should talk about what attracts them to a certain pizza parlor—it may be the location, the recommendation of someone else, the menu—if it is included—or other aspects of the ad.

93. You would check the yellow pages under "lock" and would find "locksmith." Then you would call the locksmith to come and help you unlock your car.

94. The local library; students should write the number for library. If there is more than one branch, they should write these numbers down as well.

95. Answers will vary.

96. The service numbers are generally located in the front of the phone book.

97. Some drugstores may advertise in the yellow pages as open 24 hours. Otherwise, you may call drugstores for their hours.

98. Answers will vary. Sample answers: Section A: National and World News; Section B: Local News; Section C: Business; Section D: Sports; Section E: Wheels *Note:* Some papers will have more sections; some may have fewer. Be sure students identify the overall theme of each section.

99. Answers will vary.

100. Answer will vary according to newspapers.

Daily Warm-Ups: Everyday Skills

101. Students should be able to find the main idea of the day's top news story and create a similar headline.

102.

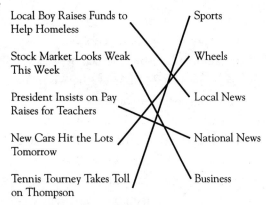

Local Boy Raises Funds to Help Homeless — National News

Stock Market Looks Weak This Week — Business

President Insists on Pay Raises for Teachers — Local News

New Cars Hit the Lots Tomorrow — Wheels

Tennis Tourney Takes Toll on Thompson — Sports

(matched to: Sports, Wheels, Local News, National News, Business)

103–105. Answers will vary.

106. Sections may include Home and Family, Comics, Parade Magazine, TV Week, Real Estate, Outdoors, Travel.

107. Students should discuss issues that may concern them or their community.

108. You look at a timetable.

109. 1. leaves Thorsenville 9:30 A.M., arrives Kate's Crossing 1:05 P.M.; leaves Thorsenville at 4:10 P.M., arrives Kate's Crossing 8:55 P.M. 2. 9:55 A.M. 3. 4:35 P.M.

110. 1. 7:30 A.M. 2. Varney to Thorsenville 3. 23 minutes

111. 1. Tuesday and Friday 2. 45 minutes 3. Monday and Friday

112. 1. Friday 2. Friday 3. 5 minutes

113. 1. These are daytime showings. 2. Rob's Revenge and Susan and the Susanettes 3. Basic Powers 4. Rob's Revenge, because it has the most number of showings

114. 1. to work as a cashier or a stockperson at Maggie's store 2. Date of Birth 3. Social

Security Number

115. 1. Students should fill in employment information. If they have not yet held a job, they should write a few sentences that describe their experience or qualifications for the job. 2. Employers want to see how qualified you are for the job. 3. A reference is a person the employer can call to see how well you worked on that job. 4. Students should fill in the name and number of someone who could help them as a reference— someone they worked or volunteered for.

116. 1. It asks for what types of reading you have been doing. 2. fiction or nonfiction; 3. Fiction is made-up stories; nonfiction is factual stories. 4. To check any other type of reading you have been doing; the implication is that all reading counts.

117. 1. Students can keep track of their assignments and see their progress. This can help remind them of what is due in the future. 2. Teachers can track how well students completed their work and how well they are keeping up with the assignments. 3. Students should think about two or three assignments they have had in the past month and how well they did on getting them in on time. Students may want to adapt this form for real use in their classroom.

118. The store can send you an e-mail to let you know they have your form. The store assumes you have e-mail because you submitted the form online. 2. Call the toll-free number. 3. so the store knows what size bikes to choose for the riders

119. Triple the recipe.

Daily Warm-Ups: Everyday Skills

120.

Breakfast	Snack	Lunch	Dinner	Snack
500	250	500	500	250

121. 1 cup mayonnaise; 1/2 cup sour cream; 6 tablespoons cream; 1 1/2 cups fresh parsley

122. 1/4 c mixed greens; 1/2 cucumber; 1/2 tomato, diced; 1/4 of a red pepper, diced; 1 tsp scallions; 1/4 c fresh lemon juice; 3/4 c oil; 1 Tbl mustard; 1/4 c grated Parmesan cheese

123. 57

124. 21

125. Answer will vary, but should include a telephone call to the doctor's office asking him or her to phone in a prescription to a nearby drugstore.

126. June 8

127. $21.40

128. You could ask for slightly less pay in exchange for benefits; you could ask for benefits after you've proved that you are a strong worker; you could ask what other people in your position do about health insurance benefits.

129. 1. 85%; 2. 75%; 3. yes

130. 24 cans of food; 6 blankets; 6 flashlights; 12 batteries (this assumes flashlights take 2 batteries each); 18 bottles of water; 12 changes of clothes

131. b

132. Answers will vary. Sample answers: 1. Your service/credit card could be shut off. 2. Bill collectors could start calling your house. 3. You could get bad credit. 4. You could have to sell something or move out of your house.

133. 1. yes 2. yes, $273; 3. Put it in a savings account.

134. d
135. $17.84 per month; $214.08 per year
136. $85.50 per year
137. d
138. Answers may include you can cut back on miscellaneous expenses set aside for this month; you can borrow some money from your savings, if you have any; you can be sure that next month's bill is less than usual; you can earn more money by working extra hours.
139. Add up the number of checks in the 6 months: 70; divide by 6 months: 11.6; multiply by $.25 = $2.92 per month.
140. $66.50; Never bounce a check again!
141. A debit transaction takes money directly out of your account. A credit card transaction goes through the credit card company and often has an additional charge attached to it, plus interest.
142. 1. b 2. c
143. Answers will vary, but may include overspending; don't find mistakes in adding or subtracting; don't know how much things cost; don't know how much money will be available for saving; can't figure out expenses each month or at the end of the year; don't know how much money you need to make.
144. $1.19 + .59 = $1.79 for 6 apples
145. 1. $28.99; 2. $10.47; 3. $3.49
146. $4.02
147. $11.80; $10.62
148. Students should name some food from each area. Then they can discuss where they most often find bargains.
149. 1. $46.97; 2. $54.02

150. $13.57
151. $61.50
152. 1. $530; 2. $44
153. Answers will vary. One option would be to take the can back in the store bag and talk to the manager about a return.
154. Answers will vary but could include to put the hood up and tie a white cloth to the door handle; remind students not to get in a car with people they don't know—if someone stops and offers to make a telephone call, that is acceptable, but remind them not to get into a car with a stranger.
155. 1. 3 hours and 4 minutes; 2. 36 minutes; 3. 4 hours and 23 minutes
156. 50 minutes
157. Students will need to research travel by bus, plane, or train. Help them with Internet searches or other ways to find timetables.
158. 25 months, or 2 years and 1 month
159. $101.50
160. $14.61
161. 3.8 miles; 3.2 miles
162. $11.70
163. $3.33
164. Answers will vary, but may include what type of climate they have; what form of money they use; what the sights to see are; what language they speak. Students will likely focus on what interests them.
165. $261.00
166. Documents might include passport, visa, medical records.
167. $8.74
168. 37.8 miles

169. Students whose languages are represented may help with pronunciation.

170–180. These questions should spark discussion about what students can say and do in difficult situations. Encourage good problem-solving tactics.

Turn downtime into learning time!

Other books in the
Daily
Warm-Ups series:

- Algebra
- Algebra II
- Analogies
- Biology
- Character Education
- Chemistry
- Commonly Confused Words
- Critical Thinking
- Earth Science
- Geography
- Geometry
- Journal Writing
- Logic
- Math Word Problems
- Mythology
- Physics
- Poetry
- Pre-Algebra
- Prefixes, Suffixes, & Roots
- Shakespeare
- Spelling & Grammar
- Test-Prep Words
- U.S. History
- Vocabulary
- World Cultures
- World History
- World Religions
- Writing